ETHICAL DEBATES

Cosmetic Surgery

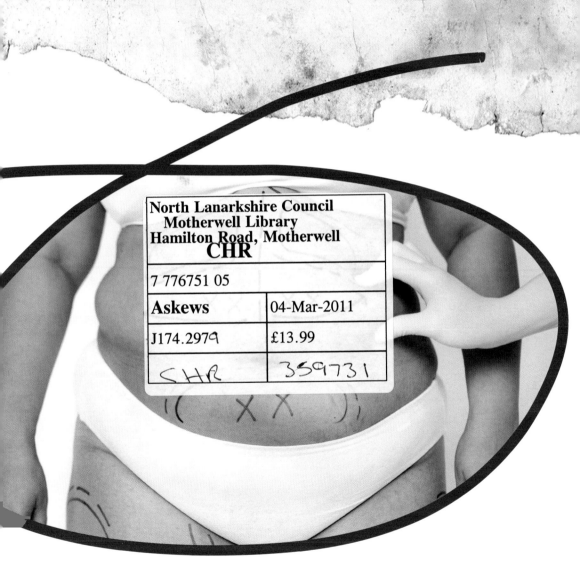

KAYE STEARMAN

WAYLAND

First published in 2009
by Wayland

Copyright © Wayland 2009

Wayland
338 Euston Road
London NW1 3BH

Wayland Australia
Level 17/207 Kent Street
Sydney NSW 2000

Commissioning editor: Jennifer Sanderson
Designer: Rita Storey
Picture researcher: Kathy Lockley
Proofreader: Susie Brooks

British Library Cataloguing in
Publication Data
 Stearman, Kaye
   Cosmetic surgery. - (Ethical debates)
   1. Surgery, Plastic - Moral and
   ethical aspects -
   Juvenile literature
   I. Title
   174.2'97952

ISBN 978 0 7502 5654 4

Printed in China

Wayland is a division of
Hachette Children's Books,
an Hachette UK company.
www.hachettelivre.co.uk

Picture acknowledgements:
The author and publisher would like to thank the
following agencies for allowing these pictures to be
reproduced: Aflo Co. Ltd/Alamy: 18; AFP/Getty
Images: 9; allOver Photography/Alamy: COVER, 24;
Avatra Images/Alamy: 27; Alessandra Benedetti/Corbis:
21; Bettmann/Corbis: 13; Black Star/Alamy: 6;Hubert
Boesl/dpa/Corbis: 23; John Chapple/Rex Features:
33;F1 online digitale Bildagentur GmbH/Alamy: 17;
Nicole Fruge/ZUMA/Corbis: 39; Getty Images: 28
Louise Gubb/Corbis: 41; Mark Henley/Panos Pictures:
30; Gary Hershorn/Reuters/Corbis: 25; Reinhard
Krause/Reuters/Corbis: 44; Milk Photographic/Corbis:
Titlepage, 43; Kazuyoshi Nomachi/Corbis: 19; Erik C.
Pendzich/Rex Features: 37; Mark Peterson/Corbis: 35
Phanie Agency/Rex Features: 38; Ryan Pyle/Corbis: 36
Ryan Pyle/None/Corbis: 42; The RAMC Muniment
Collection in the care of the Wellcome Library,
London: 8; John R. Rifkin/Lebrecht Music & Arts/
Corbis: 20; Frances M. Roberts/Alamy: 5; Santa
Barbara California Sheriff Department/Handout
/epa/Corbis: 32; Denis Sinyakov/Reuters/Corbis: 7
Sipa Press/Rex Features: 15, 29; Lourens Smak/Alamy:
16; Tom Stewart/Corbis: 26; Geoffrey Swaine/Rex
Features: 34; Janine Wiedel Photography/Alamy: 10
Every attempt has been made to clear copyright.
Should there be any inadvertent omission please
apply to the publisher for rectification.

About the consultant:
Dr Patricia Macnair is a hospital physician working in
a small rehabilitation hospital with elderly patients
who are recovering from major illness. She has a
Masters degree in Medical Ethics and Medical Law,
and has a particular interest in vulnerable patients,
end-of-life issues, palliative care, pain control, obesity
and weight loss.

Note:
The website addresses (URLs) included in this book
were valid at the time of going to press. However,
because of the nature of the Internet, it is possible
that some addresses may have changed, or sites may
have changed or closed down since publication.
While the author and publishers regret any
inconvenience this may cause the readers, no
responsibility for any such changes can be accepted
by either the authors or the publishers.

contents

Real-life case study

This case study highlights some of the issues that surround the debate on cosmetic surgery.

case study

Computers and cosmetic surgery

Miss Bimbo is not real. Like so many things today she is a virtual creation, a character in an electronic game played over the Internet. Unlike most games that are aimed at boys and adults, and feature guns, fights and car chases, Miss Bimbo is designed to target girls and involves the quest for beauty and celebrity.

In the game, each contestant has a naked, virtual character to look after. The contestant must make her character the 'hottest, coolest, most famous bimbo in the world', and to do this they must compete against other Miss Bimbos, dressing their character in sexy outfits, taking her shopping and clubbing, and making her as attractive as possible. This includes cosmetic surgery at the virtual clinic, giving her virtual breast implants and facelifts.

Miss Bimbo was developed in France in 2007 and had 1.2 million players in the first year. The game was launched in the United Kingdom (UK) in 2008, and within a few months had 200,000 players. In both countries, most players are girls aged between 9 and 16. Although the game is initially free to play, the contestants later have to pay money by sending text messages or signing up to an Internet paying-in system.

Miss Bimbo has attracted huge controversy. Parents say that it is exploitative, enabling young girls to unwittingly run up large amounts of debt on their mobile telephones as they compete to outdo fellow subscribers. Others who are against the game focus on the image of womanhood it promotes – one of consumption, stupidity, vanity and empty celebrity. The use of cosmetic surgery on the virtual characters has attracted particular attention. Critics say that it is a sinister way to get young girls to accept cosmetic surgery as a normal part of life, on the same level as getting a new dress or new haircut and where appearance is seen as more important than talent or personality.

Bill Hibberd of parents' rights group Parentkind says the game could corrupt children's innocence. 'The danger is if a nine-year-old fails to appreciate the irony and sees the bimbo as a cool role model. Then the game becomes a hazard and a menace. The danger is that after playing the game some will aspire to have breast operations and take diet pills.'

Supporters of the game point out that Miss Bimbo is, after all, just a game and does not influence real-world behaviour. Nicolas Jacquart, the designer of the web game, defends Miss Bimbo as 'harmless fun'. He says, 'It is not a bad influence on young children. They learn to take care of their bimbos. The missions and goals are morally sound and teach children about the real world.'

viewpoints

'We are not encouraging girls to have breast operations. It is just part of the game. It simply mirrors real life in a tongue-in-cheek way.'
Nicholas Jacquart, Miss Bimbo website designer

'The message [from Miss Bimbo] is clear and simple: a girl's value is in her looks, and if you're not happy with them then fix the way you look, and that's the only way you'll be happy.'

Linda Papadopoulos, psychologist

It's a fact

Michael Phelps, super-swimmer and winner of eight gold medals at the Beijing Olympics in 2008, was frequently teased about his large, sticking-out ears. He decided not to have cosmetic surgery to pin them back but used the 'immense hurt' from the teasing to motivate his swimming success. Winning was a way of answering back to his tormentors.

▼ The Digi makeover toy has been described as the 'ultimate style station for girls'. A digital photograph is placed on a computer screen and digitally manipulated, just as happens with many magazine photos. Is this innocent fun or the first step on the road to cosmetic surgery?

CHAPTER 1

Cosmetic surgery – the basics

What do you think of when you hear the words 'cosmetic surgery'? For many people, the immediate image is of an inert body, paralyzed by anaesthetics lying, on an operating table in a clinic while a doctor wields a scalpel. This image is a staple of dozens of television shows, both real and fictitious.

Another common image is of a celebrity captured in the flashbulbs, maybe at a glamorous premiere or stumbling out of a nightclub in the early hours of the morning. Millions of readers of magazines and websites eagerly wait for news of their favourite celebrity's latest forays into cosmetic surgery to make them more beautiful and desirable.

A useful definition

The term 'cosmetic surgery' is often misused and misunderstood. For many people the terms 'cosmetic surgery' and 'plastic surgery' are interchangeable. However, although cosmetic surgery is a branch of plastic surgery there are significant differences between the two.

In 2005, an expert committee in the UK reported to the Chief Medical Officer on the regulation of cosmetic surgery in the UK. The committee defined cosmetic surgery as: 'Operations and other procedures that revise or change the appearance, colour, texture, structure or position of bodily features which most would otherwise recognize to be in the broad range of what is 'normal' for that person.'

This definition raises two important points. Firstly, cosmetic surgery includes much more than surgery – which the experts described as 'invasive procedures carried out in an operating theatre under an anaesthetic'. Modern cosmetic surgery also includes other procedures such as injecting Botox

◀ A surgeon performs liposuction on an anaesthetized patient. Such operations are becoming part of modern medical practice.

or aesthetic fillers and laser treatment. However, the expert committee excluded ear and body piercing, tattooing, and other procedures that had no permanent effect, from the definition of cosmetic surgery. It did not consider the field of dentistry, where many procedures are carried out for cosmetic rather than for dental or hygienic reasons. (These procedures were governed by other laws and regulations.)

Secondly, cosmetic surgery is not about health or medical needs – it is about changing the appearance of 'normal' people. It is about people who want to improve their appearance, by removing 'bad' features or enhancing 'good' features.

In the mildest form, cosmetic surgery might be removing a mole or freckles or having ears pinned back, changes that would be unnoticeable to most people. These are common operations and are often carried out in childhood. At a more serious level, cosmetic surgery involves visible alterations, which include operations that lift and stretch the skin in a facelift or enlarge the lips with collagen injections. These are purely cosmetic procedures, usually carried out in private clinics.

Surgical operations are used to change the shape and size of the face or body, for example, a nose, a chin, breasts, buttocks or stomach. These are major operations, carried out by surgeons operating on anaesthetized patients, and where there is often a considerable recovery period. These operations are designed to make a major and permanent change to a person's appearance, sometimes in an extreme way. Increasingly common are less complex non-surgical procedures that result in temporary changes, such as smoothing the skin, removing wrinkles and plumping up lips.

▲ Actress and glamour model Pamela Anderson poses on the red carpet at an awards ceremony in 2007. How much of her body and face is real and how much of it is natural?

It's a fact

In 2007, the UK cosmetic surgery market reached a value of US$ 934 million (£493 million). Breast augmentation is one of the most popular operations, together with skin treatments such as Botox.

There were over 11.7 million cosmetic procedures in the United States in 2007. Just over 2 million were for operations, such as liposuction and breast augmentation, and 9.6 million were for non-invasive procedures, such as Botox, injectables and laser hair removal.

Cosmetic surgery in the past

Throughout history, people have tried to make themselves more attractive by painting their bodies and faces with dyes and cutting and arranging their hair.

Before the discovery of anaesthetics in the nineteenth century, body changes through surgery were rare and limited to urgent or life-saving surgery. Any surgery was extremely painful and many people died from shock or infection. The use of anaesthetics, which sent the patient into a pain-free sleep, and of sterile techniques and disinfectants that reduced infection, opened the way for the huge range of major and minor surgery that we know today, including plastic surgery.

Plastic (derived from the Greek word 'plastikos', meaning shaped or moulded) surgery is a medical speciality that uses surgical and non-surgical techniques to change the body's appearance and functions. Plastic surgery developed especially during the First and Second World Wars, as hospitals learned to reconstruct the faces and bodies of soldiers and civilians maimed and disfigured on the battleground or in bombed cities.

Today, most plastic surgery is medical and reconstructive – restoring a sick or injured person as much as possible to their former state. Common examples include repairing cleft palates on tiny babies, grafting new skin onto a burns victim, or operating on a person who has been in a road accident. Plastic surgery can have both medical and cosmetic aspects, for example giving a new breast to a woman who has lost one through cancer or removing excess weight from a severely overweight person whose life is in danger. It is the cosmetic aspects on which this book focuses.

Plastic surgery ▶
developed rapidly during wartime as doctors developed new techniques to rebuild shattered bodies and faces. These photographs show a soldier who was injured in the First World War undergoing facial reconstruction.

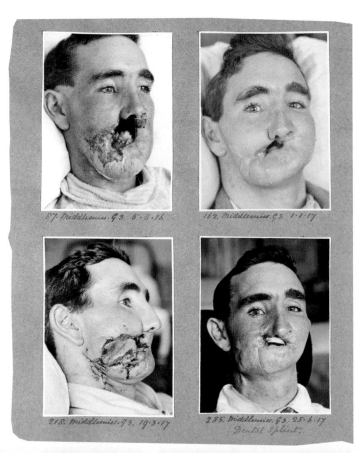

case study

From little goddess to little girl

When a little girl in India was born with four arms and four legs, her parents called her Lakshmi after the four-armed Hindu goddess of prosperity. Many of the local villagers began to worship her as a goddess. Others wanted to sell her to a circus for exhibition.

Lakshmi's condition was created in the womb. Her mother had been carrying identical twins that had failed to separate. The second, weaker twin withered, leaving her limbs joined to the stronger twin, Lakshmi. Although Lakshmi survived the birth and could function, she would never be able to walk or live a normal life.

Lakshmi's parents could not afford the reconstructive surgery she needed.

They thought carefully when a top hospital in Bangalore in southern India offered to operate on Lakshmi free of charge. The operation had never been attempted before and would be risky. Some people said that it was wrong to operate and it was Lakshmi's fate to be born as she was. Nevertheless, her parents made the decision to go ahead with the operation.

The operation took place in November 2007 with a team of 30 surgeons working for over 24 hours. They removed her extra limbs, reconstructed her lower body and transplanted a kidney from the parasitic twin to Lakshmi. The operation was successful and it will allow Lakshmi to live a new independent life, no longer a goddess or a circus attraction.

▼ Lakshmi with her parents after the operations that changed her life.

Types of surgery

Cosmetic surgery falls into two main categories: surgical and non-surgical. Surgery involves cutting into the skin, removing tissue and fat, or grafting skin usually from elsewhere on the body. Common facial cosmetic surgery includes rhinoplasty (changing the size or shape of the nose), otoplasty (reshaping the ears), blepharoplasty (eyelid surgery) and rhytidectomy (facelifts). Surgical treatments also include surgery to change the shape of a chin or cheeks. Body surgery includes resizing and reshaping women's breasts and buttocks, and liposuction, which involves removing fat.

Non-surgical treatments are more recent developments and are rapidly growing in popularity. They include chemical peels, where chemical compounds are used to remove skin problems, such as acne, spots and scars, as well as removing natural features such as freckles and wrinkles, and injecting 'fillers,' such as collagen, into skin and tissues. One of the fastest-growing treatments is the injection of Botox into the skin to make it appear smoother.

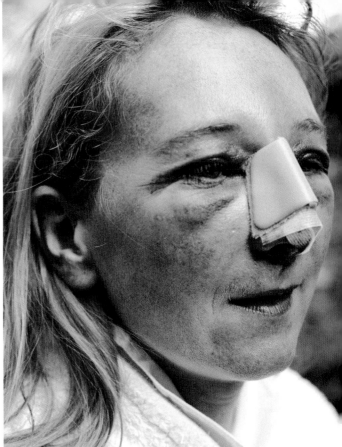

▲ This woman is recovering from a nose reshaping operation. Eventually the bandages will be removed and the bruises will fade.

Attitudes to cosmetic surgery

In the past, cosmetic surgery was aimed mainly at women, especially older and richer women who were keen to present a youthful appearance. The procedures were expensive and rarely discussed. Most of those who underwent cosmetic surgery wanted people to believe that their youthful appearance came about because of natural good looks or a healthy lifestyle.

As knowledge and techniques have expanded, prices for cosmetic surgery have fallen and many more people are prepared to undertake operations and procedures that were once seen as difficult and dangerous. Cosmetic surgery is no longer just for older women, and growing numbers of younger women and men are attempting to improve their faces and bodies with cosmetic surgery.

Perhaps the biggest change is in attitudes. No longer is cosmetic surgery always something to be done secretly or shamefacedly. Instead, the various procedures and options are openly discussed, not just between groups of friends but in magazines and on television.

For some people, changing their face or body is regarded as a normal consumer transaction, like trading in a car or having their hair done.

Cosmetic surgery is most popular in more affluent countries, where people can earn, borrow or inherit funds to pay for the procedures. Top of the list is the United States, with Brazil in second place. Cosmetic surgery is also popular in Europe and countries such as Australia, Canada, Japan and New Zealand. It has also spread to other areas, such as the Arab world, Korea and China.

Cosmetic surgery today

Although cosmetic surgery has become more common, it is still controversial and the subject of many arguments. Supporters say that it is a product of modern scientific and technological changes. Overall, it is safe and hygienic, carried out by trained and experienced practitioners at prices that are more affordable. It not only makes people look good, but it also makes them feel good. As a result those who undergo surgery have happier lives, have greater choice and more control over their destinies – and, overall, society benefits.

Critics say that much cosmetic surgery is neither safe nor properly regulated, and in many cases, is unnecessary. They point to the profitable industry built around cosmetic surgery and say that it uses unscrupulous methods to sell unrealistic dreams to young and old alike. Rather than making people happy, it feeds on their fears and insecurities about their appearance. Rather than giving them greater control over their lives, it undermines them. Critics also say that cosmetic surgery is the product of a society that does not value individuality or difference, and wants everyone to look the same.

viewpoints

'I believe in cosmetic surgery. It has everything to do with how a person feels about him or herself. There is no such thing as too much.'
Joan Rivers, comedienne and talk show host

'Plastic surgery and breast implants are fine for people who want that, if it makes them feel better about who they are. But, it makes these people, actors especially, fantasy figures for a fantasy world. Acting is about being real, being honest.'
Kate Winslet, actor and movie star

summary

▶ Cosmetic surgery is a branch of plastic surgery and has rapidly developed over the past decades.

▶ Cosmetic surgery aims to revise or change a person's 'normal' appearance.

▶ There are many types of cosmetic surgery and new procedures are developed all the time.

▶ In the past, most people were ashamed of undertaking cosmetic surgery but today, attitudes towards cosmetic surgery are more open.

▶ More and more people now turn to cosmetic surgery, especially cheaper non-surgical processes, to enhance their appearance.

▶ The majority of people undertaking cosmetic surgery are women, although there are growing numbers of men and teenagers undergoing procedures.

11

Is cosmetic surgery harmful?

Is cosmetic surgery compatible with medical ethics? In other words, is it right for doctors and surgeons to undertake operations and procedures for which there is no medical need?

Medical ethics

What are the medical ethics that govern cosmetic surgery? The most famous code of medical ethics is one of the oldest. Physicians in Ancient Greece were obliged to take an oath, known as the Hippocratic Oath, to ensure they provided good quality care and made decisions that were best for their patients. The Hippocratic Oath has been amended many times in the following 2,500 years, but many of its principles still provide an ethical basis for medical practice today.

Critics of cosmetic surgery say that unnecessary treatments are wrong and incompatible with the principles of medical ethics, especially those of beneficence, non-maleficence and justice (see below). They contend that the principle of 'do no harm' should come first. Cosmetic surgery is not a treatment for injury or illness and therefore cannot cure sickness or improve health. However, all medical procedures involve a risk, however small. Critics say that by undertaking an unnecessary procedure, a doctor is placing his or her patient at risk and therefore not acting in the patient's best interests. And when cosmetic surgery is unsatisfactory or goes wrong, as it does in some cases, then the patient's life and health is made worse, rather than better.

Some of the principles of the Hippocratic Oath have a direct relevance to modern cosmetic surgery. They include:	
Beneficence	A doctor should always do the best by their patient, balancing dangers and risks with the likely outcome.
Non-maleficence	Do no harm. A treatment should not worsen the patient's health or well-being.
Truthfulness	A patient should be fully informed of their condition and the advantages and drawbacks of any treatment offered.
Autonomy	A patient has the right to decide whether to accept or reject treatment or advice.
Justice	Using medical resources in a fair and equitable way to benefit people and society.

Supporters of cosmetic surgery reject these arguments. They point out that people knowingly take many risks in their everyday life – life itself is full of risks. They argue that today people no longer expect to follow doctors without question, but are capable of collecting information and making up their own minds about what treatments are right for them. For supporters, the ethics of cosmetic surgery focus on the principles of informed consent and autonomy (independence). They say that as long as people are able to have full information about the procedures on offer, and are not pressured to undertake unwanted or unaffordable treatment, then cosmetic surgery is consistent with medical ethics.

It's a fact

There are 20,000 plastic surgeons worldwide who belong to the International Society of Aesthetic Plastic Surgeons.

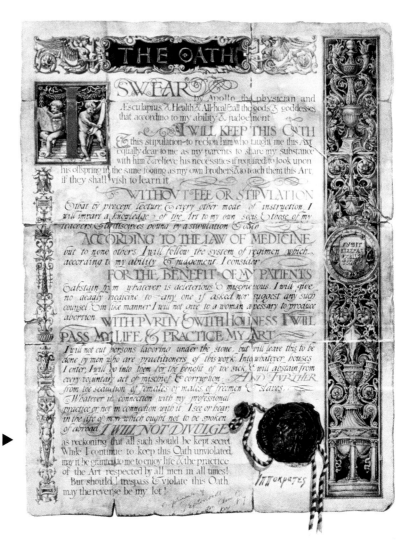

Doctors have sworn on variations of the Hippocratic Oath for many centuries. This version is elaborately written and illustrated.

Safety issues

Is cosmetic surgery safe? This is a difficult question to answer because there are many different types of cosmetic surgery and many procedures, each carrying its own risks and dangers. However, there have been many concerns about the overall safety record of cosmetic surgery.

Critics give examples where cosmetic surgery has been proved to be unsafe and created medical problems. One of the most notorious instances was the case of breast implants that contained sacs made of and filled with silicone – a type of plastic. Silicone implants were introduced in the United States in the 1960s and used for both medical and cosmetic surgery to replace or enlarge women's breasts. Over 30 years it is estimated that more than one million women were given the implants. From the beginning, there were complaints by women that they feared that the implants were making them ill – fears that were proven correct. Research showed that silicone sometimes leaked from the implants and migrated to other parts of the body and that women with implants had higher rates of cancers and other illnesses.

However, it was only in 1992 that the United States Food and Drug Administration (FDA) decided to stop the sale and use of the implants. Some women brought lawsuits against the companies that manufactured the implants. In 1994, three corporations agreed to provide US$3.7 billion (£1.85 billion) over 30 years to compensate victims in the United States (although the payments did not begin for a further ten years). The companies said that they did not believe that the implants were unsafe but that they agreed to the payments to avoid further lawsuits.

case study

The cheerleader who died

Stephanie Kuleba died on the operating table on 22 March 2008. She was only 18 years old and had been a cheerleader at her high school in Florida, United States.

The circumstances of her death made headlines across the United States: she had been undergoing breast augmentation surgery when she died. As a result, there were many questions raised about the ethics and safety of cosmetic surgery, especially on a teenager.

Stephanie's family said her operation was not purely for cosmetic reasons but to fix asymmetrical (differently sized) breasts.

They believed that the operation was both necessary and safe. Stephanie's surgeon, Dr Frederick Lukash, said that he had performed similar operations on other teenage girls and that the procedure was safe. Stephanie had apparently died from malignant hyperthermia, a rare genetic disorder brought about by anaesthesia.

But many people questioned both the general safety of cosmetic surgery and its use on teenagers. Both the American Society of Plastic Surgeons and the FDA said that patients under the age of 18, whose bodies were still developing, should not receive breast implants for cosmetic reasons.

As a result of the lawsuits and media publicity, there was a move towards higher standards and greater regulation of implant operations. Within a few years, silicone breast implants were banned, not just in the United States but also Canada, France, the UK, Japan and other countries. Today, silicone implant filling has been replaced by a saline (salt solution) filling, although the implant sac is still made of silicone.

Critics of cosmetic surgery felt that the outcome of the case supported their concerns and say that other procedures may also be unsafe, especially those where the long-term outcome is unknown. Supporters acknowledge that in the past some types of cosmetic surgery have been problematic, especially when they were not subject to the rigorous testing and regulation that was later introduced.

▼ Saline-filled silicone breast implants are now the norm in breast enlargement operations. This factory in Rio de Janerio, Brazil, is a major supplier in the city.

However, as cosmetic procedures become more common, they become ever safer. In addition, today there is more media scrutiny and consumers are much better informed than in the past. Supporters argue that today cosmetic surgery is part of the ever-advancing progress of medical science, which aims not only to cure illness but also to improve people's lives.

v i e w p o i n t s

'Some teens are more prepared for surgery than adults. We look for maturity and realistic expectations.'
Walter Erhardt, plastic surgeon, Georgia, United States

'The big problem with adolescents is that they are being operated on at the most tumultuous time in their lives. They may not recognize the permanence of what they are doing.'
David Sarwer, Center for Human Appearance, University of Pennsylvania Medical School, United States.

Safeguards

In most countries, only professional plastic surgeons are permitted to undertake the most complex operations, such as facial and body surgery. Many have years of experience, a huge amount of skill and are able to combine cosmetic surgery with reconstructive surgery. However, this is not always the case and some surgeons may not have the specialist qualifications. Information is often hard to come by, but it appears that in some countries there are few or no regulations regarding the qualifications of people who perform cosmetic operations.

More and more cosmetic surgery is non-surgical in nature. While some is still carried out by health professionals, many procedures are done by people without medical training. One example is of the injection of Botox into the facial tissues. Botox injections are often advertised as a procedure that is so quick and easy that it can be done in a lunchtime appointment in a beauty salon.

Botox

Botullinium toxin (Botox) is one of the most poisonous substances in the world. Medically, it is used to treat limb and muscle spasms and damage to vocal chords. However, today its most common use is as a 'non-surgical, mini-facelift', rather than as a medical procedure.

Injecting tiny amounts of Botox into the face temporarily paralyzes the facial muscles, reducing the contractions that cause wrinkles and, at the same time, ironing out existing ones. The treatment first became popular with ageing celebrities, keen to present a youthful face to the world. But as prices for treatment dropped, Botox became more popular, especially with younger people, even if they did not actually have any wrinkles.

Botox can indeed make people look younger and wrinkle-free, but some experts question its safety. In 2008, the

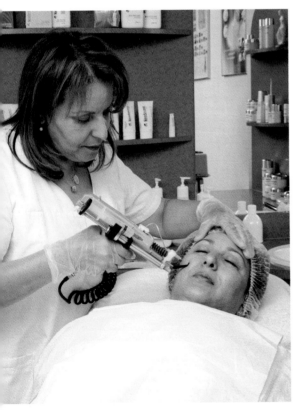

◄ A nurse administers a mesotherapy injection to a patient. Mesotherapy uses a combination of pharmaceutical substances, plant extracts and vitamins to improve the condition of skin.

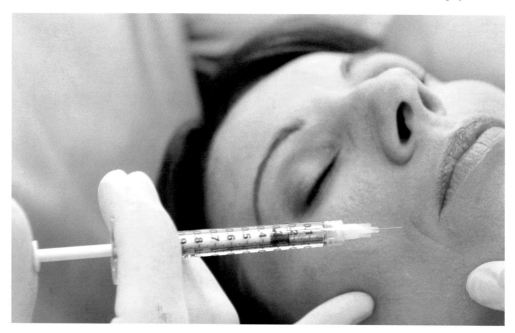

FDA investigated 16 deaths that were connected to the use of Botox, together with other cases leading to hospital treatment. Also in 2008, Italian scientists who injected Botox into rats found that it moved from the face to the brain within a few days and remained there six months later. Critics say that these events are evidence that the use of Botox is potentially unsafe and can cause harm. This is especially so if the injections are applied by a person without medical training, as has been reported at 'Botox parties', held in people's homes as a social event.

However, supporters say that the deaths in the United States were not related to cosmetic surgery and that there is no evidence that the rat experiments bear any relation to what happens with humans. Critics point out that Botox can have temporary side effects, such as droopy eyelids and a 'frozen face', and since it has been used for cosmetic surgery for only a short time (about 20 years), doctors do not yet know any long-term effects.

▲ Botox and other so-called 'new injectables' are the fastest-growing procedures in cosmetic surgery. They are easier to administer than more complex operations and the patient does not need an anaesthetic. They are also considerably cheaper than surgery. However, as yet, the long-term effects of Botox are unknown.

summary

▶ Cosmetic surgery is a controversial issue with people holding strong views on both sides.

▶ There are many medical ethical issues around cosmetic surgery, especially those about unnecessary treatment, safety and risk.

▶ After years of complaints and litigation, silicone breast implants have been ruled unsafe and are now banned in many countries.

▶ Many critics feel that there are not enough safeguards with cosmetic surgery, including Botox injections.

CHAPTER 3

Why try to change your appearance?

The overwhelming reason that people say they choose to undergo cosmetic surgery is because they believe that it will enhance their appearance – they hope that it will make them look younger, more beautiful, more desirable. Wanting to look younger and be more beautiful is not a new impulse and it is present in all cultures. Youth and beauty, whatever forms they take, seem to be universally admired.

Beauty through history

Throughout history, people have tried to beautify their faces and bodies. Most ornamentation, such as body painting, was temporary in nature. Before modern surgery, few changes could be permanent and many were extremely painful. A common example, found in many cultures, is tattooing, where coloured dyes are incised into the skin with a sharp needle.

Other examples are more extreme, although they were accepted as normal by the people who practised them. For example, in the ancient Mayan culture of Central America, a sloping forehead was considered beautiful, so babies had their heads bound tightly to ensure that the skull would flatten. Women from the Pai Dong tribe of Myanmar and Thailand lengthen their necks by wearing heavy neck bands,

◀ Girls from the Pai Dong tribe proudly display their neck bands and traditional costume. In some areas, their distinctive appearance is a tourist attraction and brings in much-needed income. However, some members of the tribe would prefer to abandon the practice of neck lengthening.

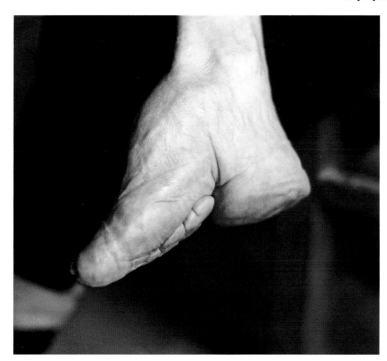

◀ This tiny deformed foot belongs to an elderly Chinese lady whose feet were bound from early childhood. The bones were broken and the toes were bent under the foot. The result was that girls could not walk properly and could only hobble short distances.

believing a longer neck to be beautiful. This weakens their spinal column and means that they cannot keep their head upright without the artificial support provided by the neck bands.

In ancient China, women with tiny feet were considered to be beautiful and desirable, and many girls from wealthier families had their feet crushed and bound to make them as tiny as possible. The process was extremely painful and resulted in grown women who could not walk more than a few steps unaided and so were confined to their homes. The practice ended only in the twentieth century when governments banned the practice of foot binding.

Even so, these examples were extreme and limited. It was not until the mid-twentieth century that medical advances made possible the types of cosmetic surgery that we know today. For supporters, cosmetic surgery is an extension of our natural impulse to ornament ourselves and improve our appearance. They say that cosmetic surgery is not very different from wearing makeup or dying hair, except that the results last longer. And, unlike the past, the procedures are safe, quick, relatively painless and are done with the full consent and knowledge of the person involved.

Critics say that cosmetic surgery is much more than enhancing or changing natural appearances, as people do when they apply makeup. It is much more drastic, costly and dangerous. The fact that it is often permanent is not an advantage, especially when people do not like the outcome. Opponents also point out that there are different ideas of beauty, and that in the modern world these change fast to reflect fashion, so what looks good today may not look as good in five or ten years' time. Critics also say that real beauty is about individuality – what makes people different from each other – yet cosmetic surgery aims to make people look similar and commonplace.

Looking younger

In today's Western society, youth and beauty are valued highly. Although everyone ages, middle age is no longer seen in terms of maturity and experience nor is old age represented as a time of wisdom. Not surprisingly, many people do not want to grow older – they want to remain young and desirable for as long as possible, and they believe that cosmetic surgery will help them to achieve this.

Traditionally, cosmetic surgery has been aimed at older and middle-aged women and this is still the industry's largest target market. Although cosmetic surgery cannot actually make middle-aged women look like teenagers, it can remove some signs of ageing and make them appear younger.

Facelifts and Botox can make the skin smoother and remove lines and wrinkles, Collagen can plump up thinning lips, while liposuction can make the skin smoother and remove wrinkles, and 'tummy tucks' remove the 'middle-age spread' from the hips and stomach.

The most prominent consumers of cosmetic surgery are people in the public eye, such as actors, singers, models and socialites, whose appearance is crucial to their careers. Young models on the catwalk and in fashion shoots model clothes that are aimed at older and richer women.

However, a much larger group of consumers includes women who want to look younger and more attractive. In addition, increasing numbers of older men are turning to cosmetic surgery, although usually for less drastic procedures than their female counterparts. The reasons are generally personal but they also relate to public perceptions. For example, younger and more attractive people may have more opportunities for better jobs and higher salaries, especially in jobs that deal with the public.

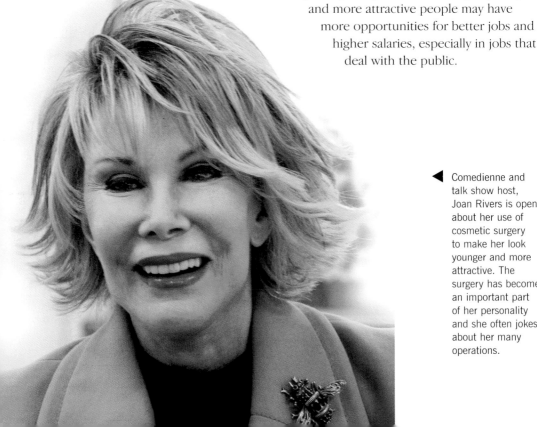

◄ Comedienne and talk show host, Joan Rivers is open about her use of cosmetic surgery to make her look younger and more attractive. The surgery has become an important part of her personality and she often jokes about her many operations.

It's a fact

It is estimated that plastic surgeons and dermatologists administer over 20,000 cosmetic injections each week day in the United States. The injections aim to remove wrinkles and skin imperfections, enhance facial appearance and remove the signs of ageing.

Supporters say that cosmetic surgery can help older people to achieve youthful looks, making them more interesting and desirable to their partners and employers. Today, older people live longer and are more active, and because they feel young, they also want to look attractive and youthful. In essence, cosmetic surgery is only one step on from dying their hair to hide the grey, wearing makeup or dressing attractively. Why should they not spend their own hard-earned money on something that makes them look and feel good?

Critics say that far from helping older people, in the long run cosmetic surgery can harm them. Those who undergo surgery may look younger from a distance but on closer inspection, tiny scars and other tell-tale signs of surgery can be seen. Furthermore, treatments such as facelifts and Botox not only pull the skin tightly and give a 'frozen face' effect, but they also remove any signs of individuality, such as laughter lines.

Many people believe that genuine weight problems can and should be resolved by eating healthier food and taking more exercise, rather than 'nip and tuck' operations. Critics also say that there is nothing wrong with looking older – surely people should aim for a society that accepts people for the age they are, not how youthful they look?

▲ In 2004, Italian Prime Minister Silvio Berlusconi, then aged 68, went missing from the limelight for a few weeks. He returned with a hair transplant and eyelid surgery. Many people were critical of his attempt to turn back the years but others saw it as a sign of his energy and vigour.

viewpoints

'As soon as I spot something dragging, sagging or bagging, I get nipped, bumped and tucked.'
Dolly Parton, country and western singer

'I would never have plastic surgery. My mother and mother-in-law lived to a very old age and their faces are maps of their lives – why would you not want that?'
Kate Mosse, novelist

Being perfect

While middle-aged men and women use cosmetic surgery to maintain a youthful appearance, the fastest-growing group of consumers of cosmetic surgery are younger women, in their 20s and 30s. In many ways this is not surprising. In many Western countries, younger women are better off than ever before. They are more highly educated, have good jobs and are healthier. Yet, many of these same women want more from life. They want to look as good as they can and see cosmetic surgery as a means to reach this goal.

For these women it is not really about looking younger, although they are still keen to remove wrinkles and other signs of ageing. It is much more about enhancing and perfecting their appearance. In this they are inspired by the celebrity role models they see in magazines, on films and in television programmes. Some of these celebrities admit to having cosmetic surgery and others deny it, although most have access to beauty treatments far beyond the budgets of ordinary women.

The most popular surgery for younger women is changing the size and shape of their faces and bodies, especially their noses and breasts. Critics say that this is more about fashion than beauty. For example, today's Western society sees small, upturned noses as beautiful, but portraits of past beauties, for example in ancient Rome, show many with large and prominent noses. Similarly, it is normal for women's breasts to come in all shapes and sizes but today's revealing fashions mean that prominent rounded breasts are fashionable, even though they may look extreme or unnatural.

Supporters point out that in a competitive world, good looks can be crucial and young people are keen to compete and stay ahead in employment and their social lives – so why not use cosmetic surgery to achieve this? For example, it is reported that in China a young woman who is regarded as especially attractive is much more likely to get a well-paid job than an equally qualified young woman who is not seen as attractive, and that many young women are turning to cosmetic surgery in the hope of widening their employment opportunities.

Opponents dispute this. They say that rather than contentment, cosmetic surgery at an early age creates discontent. For example, breast implants need to be replaced every few years, leading to more scars and tighter, less natural-looking skin. They say that young people are the ones who least need to change their appearance – youth and vitality should be enough in themselves.

Even some supporters of cosmetic surgery feel that younger people should hesitate before undertaking surgery in order to see how their faces and bodies develop over time.

It's a fact

Increasing numbers of teenagers are prepared to undertake cosmetic surgery. In 2003, almost 336,000 United States teenagers aged 18 or under, had some kind of cosmetic surgery, an increase of 50 per cent over 2002.

According to wedding magazine, *You and Your Wedding*, 7 per cent of British women plan to have a nose operation, 8 per cent intend to have a breast enlargement and 5 per cent to have a breast reduction before their wedding.

case study

Red-carpet blues

It is a badly kept secret that some of Hollywood's biggest stars resort to cosmetic surgery to enhance their appearance and maintain their youthful looks.

The greatest pressure is often on older women. The film industry prefers younger stars and once a woman is over 40, no matter how talented an actress, she is less likely to be cast in a starring role. This is much less true of men, although some have also apparently had cosmetic surgery.

While some celebrities are open about their use of Botox, facelifts and other types of cosmetic surgery, most prefer to talk about their healthy diet and strict exercise and fitness regime. It seems that many fans also prefer to believe that their favourite star's glowing appearance is not aided by cosmetic surgery.

Actress Demi Moore is reported to have spent US$300,000 (£150,000) on cosmetic surgery. This included breast implants, liposuction, brow uplifts, chemical facial peels, collagen injections and cosmetic dental surgery – she allegedly even had surgery on her 'saggy knees'. She also employed a series of advisors, including a nutritionist, yoga instructor and personal advisor to ensure that she was fit and healthy while following a rigorous exercise regime.

But four years after the surgery, she says that although she likes her appearance and is in great shape, she is still not playing the leading roles she once enjoyed. Now she says that it is time to speak out against ageism – discrimination against older people – in the movie industry.

▲ Demi Moore on the red carpet – looking good is part of the job description of a movie star.

summary

▶ People have tried to enhance their appearance throughout history and in many societies.

▶ Most people who undertake cosmetic surgery do so to change or enhance their appearance.

▶ The largest market for cosmetic surgery is older women, but increasing numbers of younger women and men are now undergoing cosmetic surgery.

CHAPTER 4

Looking good, feeling good?

If people are happy with their appearance they are more likely to feel good in themselves and content with their life and surroundings. If they are unhappy with their appearance, then they may lack confidence and have low self-esteem. Many people who have cosmetic surgery say that it has changed their life by raising their self-esteem and making them happier and more confident.

Confidence and self-esteem

For many supporters of cosmetic surgery, confidence and self-esteem is the strongest argument in its favour – although the surgery changes a person's appearance, in doing this, it changes a person's attitude to life and how they feel about themselves. If a person is unhappy or upset, if they are being teased and bullied about their appearance, then they lose confidence and their self-esteem plummets. For example, a teenage girl may feel that her nose is the wrong shape. A young woman may believe her breasts are too small or too large. A mother may say that her partner no longer desires her now that she has put on weight after childbirth. And it seems that men, especially young men, increasingly face similar insecurities. By improving their appearance, cosmetic surgery brings back people's confidence and self-esteem and enables them to better deal with other problems that they might have.

▲ Measuring up for a new face – a cosmetic surgeon marks a woman's face to indicate where he will need to cut into her skin.

For some people, cosmetic surgery does seem to make a big difference to the way they regard themselves. Their self-esteem rises and because they are more confident and outgoing, they are more likely achieve success in their relationships, work and family life. The changes in their appearance may be small ones, in fact many people may not even realize that they have had surgery, but the positive effects are apparent to all.

Critics point out that happiness really does not have that much to do with looks. It is just as much to do with personality and the way people live their lives. Many people who are not especially good looking are happy and confident because they do not place as much emphasis on appearance but on other things, such as family, friends, hobbies, sports, education, work or travel. On the other hand, those who place greater value on their appearance are likely to be unsatisfied, constantly attempting to improve their looks and comparing themselves to others.

▲ Movie star Kate Winslet says that she would not have cosmetic surgery because as an actor she needs to be real and honest.

case study

A mother's 'tummy tuck' cure

After giving birth to two healthy children, Maria should have been happy and confident, but she certainly did not feel that way. Once, she had been slim and willowy but after the two births she put on weight. What really depressed her was her unsightly, flabby tummy. Maria said: 'It was like turkey skin stretched over an old mattress – just disgusting.'

Maria's confidence plunged and she lost her self-esteem. Once she had loved wearing fashionable clothes but she began dressing in baggy tops and tracksuit bottoms.

Her husband saw how unhappy she was, but nothing he said helped to make her feel better. In despair, she went to her doctor to ask for antidepressant drugs. To her surprise, however, he referred her to a surgeon who suggested a 'tummy tuck'.

The liposuction operation removed two kilograms of skin and flesh around her stomach area and made an immediate difference to her figure. Once again Maria could wear the clothes she wanted to. But the real difference was to the way she felt. 'Now I am brimming with confidence and no longer ashamed of the way I look', she said.

▲ A person with emotional or mental problems may turn to a therapist to help them face up to their fears and insecurities. For many people, the 'talking cure' is the best solution.

Solving emotional problems

Some people believe that cosmetic surgery will do more than raise their confidence. They hope that by changing their appearance they can overcome the emotional and mental problems that blight their lives. But can cosmetic surgery really solve people's emotional and psychological problems or does it raise false hopes?

Critics argue that people's beliefs in the life-changing powers of cosmetic surgery are often unrealistic. Rather than deal with underlying problems, they are deceived into thinking that changing their appearance will change their lives. Instead of cosmetic surgery, critics say it is better to treat a person with emotional problems in other ways, for example through counselling or therapy, with drugs, or even with improved diet and exercise.

Many supporters of cosmetic surgery agree that, in itself, cosmetic surgery is not a cure for deep-seated problems. Responsible doctors and other health professionals should listen carefully to potential patients and explain exactly what surgery can and cannot do. If they feel that it will not bring benefits or the person has unrealistic expectations then they should not go ahead with the procedure. However, this is not always the case. Sometimes a person is so determined to have surgery that they will go from doctor to doctor, until one eventually agrees to operate.

Critics point out that while cosmetic surgery can correct imperfections and make people look younger, these effects are not permanent. What happens later, when the person ages and the effects of the surgery are no longer so apparent? Will they then have further treatments?

Although many people are happy with the results of their treatment, there are others who say that cosmetic surgery has not helped them. Although their appearance has changed, they are still not happy or confident. Critics contend that sometimes cosmetic surgery can actually undermine a person's sense of well-being. If they do not have it, they feel inadequate and if they do, they are perpetually unsatisfied. However, supporters say that cosmetic surgery can be the first step towards change – by improving appearance, people will have the confidence to tackle other emotional problems.

viewpoints

'What else the surgery has done is open up doors and avenues within myself that I had issues with. It made me grow up a bit and put things in perspective about what's important and what isn't. I'm not saying surgery is important, but it was the best thing for me. It has changed my life around.'
Adam Millard, who underwent cosmetic surgery in 2005

'I just turned 50, and for my birthday I gave myself a facelift. I thought it would re-energize me but it's only made me feel worse about myself and about growing older. My husband and I split up, and I don't get to see my kids as often as I'd like. I've become really focused on my physical appearance, and I'm scared now because this facelift hasn't made me feel any better.'
DH, writing to an agony aunt, Seattle, 2008

▼ A cosmetic surgeon shows a patient saline-filled silicone breast implants of different sizes.

Former pop star Pete Burns gained new fame when he appeared on the reality television show Celebrity Big Brother UK, 2006. He has had extensive cosmetic surgery to his face, including several nose jobs, cheek implants and injections into his lips. In 2006, he revealed that he had 18 months of reconstructive surgery after a procedure on his lips went wrong. In 2007, he said that he was planning to sue the surgeon involved for $US2 million (£1 million) damages.

Extreme cosmetic surgery

Some people have cosmetic surgery again and again. Changing their appearance becomes the driving force of their life. Often it starts as an attempt to improve themselves for professional reasons, for example a model or actress may have her nose straightened or lips enlarged, so that she photographs better or wins a coveted role in a film or stage production. Often, people who have had surgery once believe that their appearance can be further enhanced, so they have more surgery, and more still. After a while, they embrace the changes as part of their personality.

Is this self-expression or an obsession? Angela Diamarchi, a Brazilian model and samba dancer, says that her changing appearance is her life's work. Over 15 years, from the age of 21, she has had more than 40 operations. One operation involved having nylon wires implanted in her eyes to make her look Japanese, to celebrate one hundred years of Japanese migration to Brazil. Her passion for surgery has made her a celebrity in Brazil.

Some people use cosmetic surgery as a way to escape their past. For example, following a painful divorce at the age of 50, Jocelyn Wildenstein, a New York socialite, decided she wanted to resemble the lynxes and cheetahs she so admired. In the following years she reportedly spent US$2 million (£1 million) on surgery to turn herself into 'cat woman'. In doing so, she became a minor celebrity herself.

Some of the strongest arguments against cosmetic surgery are that it caters to people who are addicted to surgery or are mentally ill. One of the most prominent problems is body dysmorphic disorder (BDD), where a person is obsessed by his or her appearance. When BDD people look in the mirror they see (or imagine), a physical defect, perhaps to their skin, nose, stomach or other body part. Some people with BDD spend hours grooming themselves, while others become depressed and withdrawn. Some see cosmetic surgery as the only solution and will pursue it relentlessly, whatever the physical or financial costs.

Supporters of cosmetic surgery point out that these are extreme or rare cases. People with BDD are seen by some experts as mentally ill people who seek unnecessary medical treatment. A qualified and experienced cosmetic surgeon will recognize this and refuse to operate as it would be unethical. However, a determined person may seek out an unethical doctor or an unqualified person to undertake the surgery. Supporters say that the vast majority of people who have cosmetic surgery do not have BDD or suffer from mental illness, and it is wrong to judge them by reference to extreme cases.

▲ Jocelyn Wildenstein, a New York socialite, has used cosmetic surgery to turn herself into 'cat woman', at a huge financial cost.

It's a fact

University of California Professor of Psychiatry, Dr Jamie Feusner, says that an estimated 1 to 2 per cent of people around the world have BDD. The cause of the disorder may be genetic and sometimes runs in families.

summary

▶ Many people who have cosmetic surgery say that they do so to increase their confidence and self-esteem as well as improve their appearance.

▶ People who have unrealistic expectations of cosmetic surgery can suffer emotional and mental damage.

▶ A small minority of people have extreme forms of cosmetic surgery, and some become addicted to it.

CHAPTER 5

Selling cosmetic surgery

Like all businesses, clinics and other treatment centres have to inform potential consumers of the types of services they have available. Cosmetic surgery is advertised in all sorts of ways, in the press, on the radio, on television and on the Internet. Magazines aimed at women, with their emphasis on beauty and glamour, are prime advertising vehicles. There are even magazines, both online and on the newsstand, such as *Cosmetic Surgery Answers*, that focus exclusively on cosmetic surgery.

Advertising

One of the most popular advertising techniques is showing photographs of the same person, usually a woman, before and after treatment. In the 'before'

photograph, the woman often looks depressed, with lank hair and no makeup and wears frumpy clothes. However, in the after photograph, she is miraculously transformed, not just with her new nose, breasts or stomach, but a new hairstyle, well-applied makeup and flattering, fashionable clothes.

There have been reports from several countries of the use of unethical advertising. In 1999, authorities in New South Wales, Australia, decided to clamp down on misleading advertising. This included airbrushed before and after photographs, where it was reported that some 'after' photographs even showed different models, deceiving people about what can be achieved.

▼ Before and after photographs are commonly used in the cosmetic surgery industry – but is it fair comparison or misleading advertising?

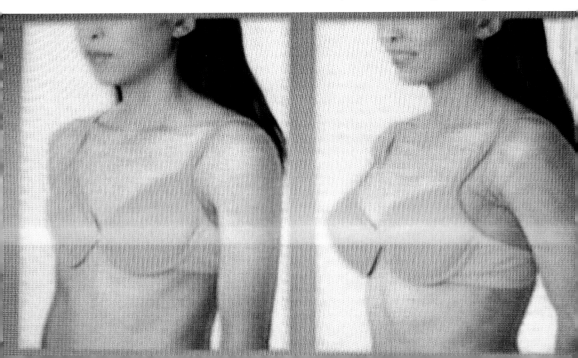

In 2007, a report by the UK consumer's association, Which?, revealed that some leading clinics were using illegal advertisements, including offering two-for-one discounts whereby women were offered reduced prices if they would agree to two procedures rather than just one or sign up for operations by a certain date. The trade association for the cosmetic surgery industry admitted that it had broken its own agreed rules against hard-sell advertising.

Worldwide web

By far the most widespread and popular form of advertising today is through the Internet. Since the 1990s, the growth of the worldwide web and quicker Internet connections to homes and businesses has opened a global marketplace for advertising all sorts of products and services, including cosmetic surgery. Setting up a website is an easy and cheap way to reach new consumers.

How reliable is the Internet? While most countries have some form of regulation

v i e w p o i n t s

'In the corporate world, there's a lot of emphasis on image, and image goes with self-confidence. I think a lot of people do invest money in improving their looks because they feel this is one way they can go up the corporate ladder.'
Antonio Armani, United States cosmetic surgeon, 2008

'It is an unfortunate circumstance that you can spend an hour with a patient treating them for diabetes and hypertension and make US$100 (£50), or you can do Botox and make US$2,000 (£1,000) in the same time.'
Dr Eric C. Parlette, United States dermatologist, 2008

of advertising in the press, on radio and on television, Internet advertising is generally unregulated. Critics point out that the lack of regulation and ease of access means that many cosmetic surgery advertisements are unethical, untruthful, dishonest and often misleading. Advertising sets out to sell a false image and is usually designed to appeal to people who are uninformed, naïve or insecure.

For people who want cosmetic surgery, the Internet has opened up a world of choice, including the option of travelling abroad for surgery. While some advertising may be misleading, supporters point out that today's consumers have grown up with advertising and they well understand the techniques used by advertisers. They also say that reputable businesses will not allow their good name to be sullied by dishonest and unethical advertising.

Blogs and chatrooms

The Internet blogs and chatrooms provide a discussion forum for people who have already had cosmetic surgery or are considering whether they should go ahead with surgery. Participants write about their own experiences, good and bad, ask and answer questions and recommend doctors and clinics in their own country or abroad. Many people believe that the best recommendations come through word of mouth from people living lives similar to their own. The Internet provides a platform where people can listen to different voices and determine whether cosmetic surgery is right for their needs.

For supporters these are very positive developments. However, critics point out that not all of the discussion forums are unbiased, and some are sponsored by, or accept advertising from, commercial clinics and practices.

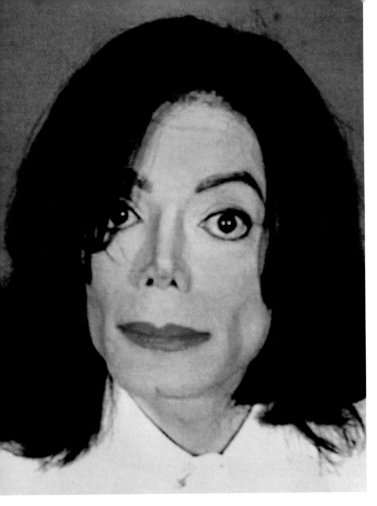

Because celebrities are constantly photographed, the world can see the changes in their appearance and often people judge them harshly.

Cynics say that celebrities undergo surgery mainly for career reasons, which are necessary in an increasingly competitive world that values appearance above talent and experience. However, few celebrities would admit this motivation. They are much more likely to say that they 'did it for me' – to fulfil a long-standing ambition to correct some defect in their appearance or to boost their confidence or self-esteem, or even just because they have have the money to do it.

The media and celebrity

The power of celebrity, promoted through the media, is one of the most important aspects of selling cosmetic surgery. Many celebrities have had cosmetic surgery to make them look younger, prettier and more photogenic. While once this was seen as a shameful secret, today, more and more celebrities are willing to admit that they have 'gone under the knife' and talk openly about their motives and experiences.

Michael Jackson is one-such celebrity. Over the years, he has undergone operations to completely change most of his facial features, including lightening his skin and altering the shape of his nose. However, he is only one of many celebrities who have followed a similar route.

Celebrities have been instrumental in promoting cosmetic surgery as a lifestyle choice. For their many fans, their choice is something to be emulated. If a celebrity can have a facelift, a breast enlargement or a tummy tuck, why should one of their fans not do the same? Maybe some of the celebrity's star quality will rub off on them, too? Magazines and websites make it easy to follow the latest trends in treatments and procedures. Supporters say that people's desire to follow celebrity is a natural impulse, but critics feel that it merely encourages unrealistic, often impossible, aspirations.

case study

My Beautiful Mommy

Dr Michael Salzhauer is a plastic surgeon based in Florida in the United States. His private clinic specializes in a range of cosmetic surgery procedures, including facelifts, tummy tucks, skin peels and Botox injections. Dr Salzhauer also appears regularly on television and radio and in magazines as an expert advisor on cosmetic surgery.

In 2008, he published a book for children called *My Beautiful Mommy*. The book looks at so-called 'mummy makeovers', which are one of the most popular areas of cosmetic surgery. Women who have given birth say that they feel rundown and less attractive than before they had their children and so turn to cosmetic surgery to make their faces younger and their bodies trimmer.

Dr Salzhauer says that children can find their mother's cosmetic surgery a stressful and scary experience. His book aims to help children cope with the process of cosmetic surgery, so that children are not frightened by the bandages and bruises that are present after an operation, or by their mother's changed appearance.

Opponents of cosmetic surgery are scornful of Dr Salzhauer's motive. They say that his aim is to introduce impressionable children to the ideas around cosmetic surgery at an early age so that they grow up thinking that it is a 'natural' and 'normal' experience. In other words, it is another way of selling cosmetic surgery to young and vulnerable future consumers.

◀ *My Beautiful Mommy* was published in 2008. The book sets out to explain cosmetic surgery to young children.

Makeover shows

The media promote cosmetic surgery in other ways, too. One recent trend has been through reality television and makeover shows. Once makeovers were confined to upgrading and decorating homes and cars. Now individuals can have the same treatment.

The shows often have similar formats where a person, nearly always a woman, is deemed to be rundown, unattractive, undesirable or simply too old, by themselves or others, and so agrees to let a team of expert stylists, hairdressers, surgeons, dentists and dermatologists improve her appearance. At first, this simply meant applying makeup, a new hairstyle and flattering clothing but the programmes soon expanded to include cosmetic procedures, such as chemical peels and

▲ Some makeover shows use cosmetic surgery to improve a participant's appearance but others, like this one hosted by Gok Wan, rely on flattering makeup and clothes and a positive attitude.

Botox, and then to surgery, sometimes major surgery, often in multiple operations, including eyebrow lifts, nose reshaping and teeth implants.

There has been a mixed reaction to these shows. For many supporters of cosmetic surgery they give a valuable account of the processes by which ordinary people can enhance their appearance, and the positive impact that it can have on their lives. They point out that the people on these shows agree to participate – in fact there is often fierce competition to be chosen – and agree to all the procedures. In return, they get thousands of dollars, or pounds, worth of cosmetic surgery free of change. They are nearly always satisfied with their new appearance, and their confidence soars.

Critics say that such shows turn cosmetic surgery into entertainment and are degrading and exploitative, focusing on vulnerable people who need counselling and therapy rather than cosmetic surgery. They fear that some people are pressured into taking part while others are so determined to be on television that they will agree to any conditions. The friends and family members who nominate each participant must comment on their appearance in negative terms, often being cruel and unkind, rather than supportive and encouraging. The outcomes have not always been good, sometimes leading to a breakdown in family relations and, in one extreme case, to the suicide of a woman who was deeply ashamed of the negative remarks she had made about her sister.

Some supporters, including cosmetic surgeons themselves, feel that these shows can go too far, either by focusing on extreme makeovers as opposed to more subtle changes, or by pressuring people into undertaking procedures that they

▲ The makeover begins before the mirror with an examination of what looks wrong and how it can be changed. But is it right to resort to cosmetic surgery to turn back the years?

would not normally want or could not afford. They point out that audience numbers have waned, at least in the United States, and the more extreme shows are no longer being screened. On the other hand, the shows are still popular in many countries around the world and many people are still keen to participate.

It's a fact

Dr John Persing of the Yale School of Medicine reported that according to a study, the more people watch celebrity makeover shows, the more they become interested in plastic surgery. The study also showed that cosmetic surgery reality television shows influenced both the expectations and choices of potential cosmetic surgery patients.

summary

▶ Cosmetic surgery businesses advertise their services widely, in the press, radio and television and on the Internet.

▶ Government agencies and consumer organizations have criticized the use of unethical and misleading advertising by cosmetic surgery businesses.

▶ Makeover shows on television and celebrity endorsement have given huge publicity to cosmetic surgery and helped to make it more acceptable.

CHAPTER 6

The business of beauty

One of the principles of medical ethics, discussed in chapter 2, is justice. This refers to using precious medical resources in a fair way to benefit individual people and society. Priority should be given to treatments for serious and life-threatening diseases rather than conditions that are less important or unnecessary to treat.

Prices and profits

Cosmetic surgery is not seen as a medical priority. Although some cosmetic surgery is carried out in government health services (usually when doctors judge that it will substantially benefit a person's health or well-being), most cosmetic surgery is provided and paid for in private hospitals and clinics. Some supporters of cosmetic surgery feel that it should be more available in public health systems, but many would agree that this would not be the best use of scarce medical resources.

It's a fact

In 2007, the German government said that patients in Germany who have suffered complications as a result of cosmetic surgery, tattoos or piercing could soon end up having to pay for the treatment themselves and that doctors should report these cases to health insurers.

This can also be a dilemma for plastic surgery specialists. Most enter the profession because they believe that they will benefit individuals and society. Some surgeons work only in the public sector, while others undertake a mixture of private and public work, sometimes subsidizing essential operations by charging extra for private cosmetic work.

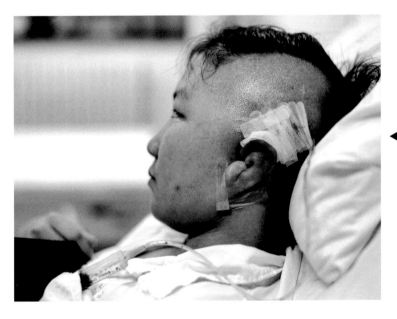

◀ An operation of any kind can be a difficult and risky experience, even when performed by expert surgeons in high-tech facilities. Critics of cosmetic surgery feel that unnecessary operations take needless risks with people's lives and health.

Private surgery is often very convenient. Most big towns and cities have clinics that carry out operations at a time to suit the customer's needs. Supporters point out that payment for private services encourages competition and choice and that this is good for consumers. With increasing demand, cosmetic surgery has become big business.

While the cost of many treatments has dropped in recent years, cosmetic surgery is not cheap. Customers pay thousands of dollars, pounds or euros for surgery such as nose reshaping, breast enlargements or reductions, or liposuction. Critics say that cosmetic surgery is exploitative – people pay high prices for unnecessary procedures. Some save up for years or take out large loans to pay for their treatment. And once they have had one procedure, they may be pressured to return for a second or third time, with costs continuing to mount.

Demand for cosmetic surgery, like other goods and services, is also affected by the economic situation. When times are good and money is easy to come by, people are happy to splash out on luxury goods, such as designer clothes, sports cars and cosmetic surgery. However, during a recession, people are likely to favour essential goods. Although the demand for cosmetic surgery procedures had been climbing for several years, by 2007, a worldwide economic slowdown was affecting the market for cosmetic surgery. Clinics reported that many people were cancelling or postponing cosmetic surgery or switching from major operations, such as facelifts and nose reshaping, to cheaper procedures such as Botox or other injectables.

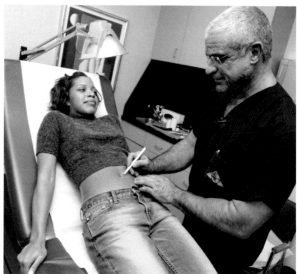

▲ Belly-button surgery to change the appearance of a patient's navel is fast becoming popular with 18 to 35 year-old women who like to show off their midriffs. The surgery takes about one hour to perform and costs about US$2,500 (£1,250).

case study

The high cost of surgery

In 2007, Roma asked her bank for a loan to finance her cosmetic surgery. She wanted her nose remodelled. She said, 'My family and friends said my nose was fine but I had been teased about it at school. When I read about nose remodelling in a celebrity magazine, I thought that I could have it done. My nose job cost US$7,200 (£3,600) and I am very happy with the result.'

The problem was that Roma was in no position to repay the money she had borrowed. She is a single mother with a young daughter and her only income was state benefits. She paid the first few monthly repayments but nothing more. Now she is thousands of pounds in debt –all for a new nose.

Regulating cosmetic surgery

Consumer organizations, which aim to protect the rights of consumers, say that whatever the arguments for or against cosmetic surgery, consumers have a right to expect good business practice and high standards.

This includes a proper health examination and full explanation of the procedures beforehand, safe procedures carried out by trained and experienced staff in hygienic conditions, proper aftercare and prompt action in response to problems. In addition, businesses should not be involved in misleading advertising or dubious sales tactics. Prices should also be clear and transparent.

Some consumer organizations have investigated the cosmetic surgery industry, often with shocking results.

In 2007, Which? investigated 20 leading UK-based clinics, with researchers posing as potential customers. It found that 'bad practice' was widespread, a view later backed by the head of the industry's own trade association and the President of the British Association of Aesthetic Plastic Surgeons. Among the violations were illegal advertising, hard-sell tactics, inadequate consultations, and pressure on patients to undertake extra operations, even if they were unwanted or unnecessary. They also found that unqualified staff

▼ It is vital that anyone considering cosmetic surgery should have the correct information and doctors should be willing and able to answer queries clearly and fully.

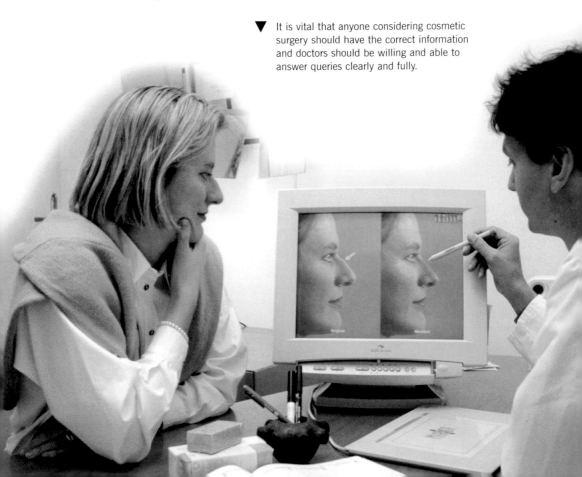

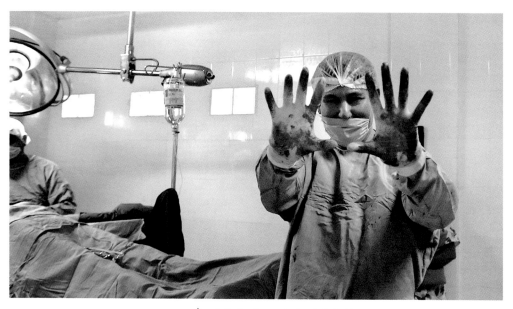

▲ A doctor in a private clinic in Nuevo Larado, Mexico, close to the US border operates on a patient. Each year thousands of people cross the border from Texas to have cosmetic surgery procedures that cost a third of similar procedures in the United States.

administered Botox, although this should be done only by doctors, dentists and some specially qualified nurses.

In many countries, government authorities are also taking action. In Australia in 2008, governments decided to act after reports of botched operations and unethical selling tactics aimed especially at young and vulnerable people. As a result, the Queensland government banned all cosmetic surgery for those under 18 years old and other states are said to be following their lead.

Many organizations in the cosmetic surgery industry recognize the harm that is being done by unqualified staff. In 2007, the death of a young woman undergoing a liposuction operation in Ontario, Canada, led to the College of Physicians and Surgeons of Ontario investigating 16 family doctors. They found that the doctors were undertaking high-risk operations in private

clinics although they lacked the specialist qualifications. Under proposed new rules, the title 'surgeon' would be reserved for doctors certified as surgical specialists by recognized medical bodies. The College of Physicians and Surgeons also laid down rules for advertising, banning reference to specific drugs or equipment as well as testimonials from patients or 'superlative statements', such as claiming fast or dramatic weight loss.

For many people these are welcome moves, showing that the industry recognizes that some business practices have been misleading and unethical, and have resulted in unsafe procedures and damaged patients. However, opponents of cosmetic surgery point out that there is a long history of unethical practice in cosmetic surgery and ask whether self-regulation (that is, by the industry itself) is enough or whether tougher government action is needed.

A global business

Cosmetic surgery is now a global business and procedures are available in many countries to meet the growing demand. Sometimes this happens in surprising places. For example, women in Saudi Arabia, who wear all-enveloping veils outside their family home, are keen consumers of cosmetic surgery. In China, growing wealth and a greater emphasis on female beauty has seen young city women encouraged to develop more 'Western', features, with double eyelid surgery being especially popular. In Brazil, operations to enhance and enlarge the buttocks are very popular, as these are considered to be the sexiest part of the female body.

A growing trend is cosmetic surgery tourism, where people travel overseas for treatment. The main reason is financial, as costs are often much lower, especially in less economically developed countries that also have good private health facilities. Other people travel in order to have operations that are considered to be dangerous or experimental – maybe doctors have refused to operate because they fear for a person's mental or physical health. Treatment is often combined with a holiday, perhaps at a beach resort or a safari park, although there is often not much fun to be had if someone is recovering from an operation.

Americans and Canadians seeking surgery abroad often head for Mexico or the Caribbean, and similarly Australians head for Southeast Asia. Many Western Europeans go to cheaper Eastern European countries or to Asia. Most often, people seek recommendations from others who have had treatments or from doctors in their home country, some of whom have links with clinics abroad.

However, the real growth in the market has come from the Internet, which has opened up a global marketplace. With a few clicks of a computer mouse, a potential customer can view options in hundreds of clinics in dozens of countries.

Supporters of cosmetic surgery say that this worldwide market is helpful. Not only does it enable greater choice but it also means that surgery is now more affordable to a wider group of people. Many supporters also point out that cosmetic surgery tourism supports the tourist industry in the host countries, as well as subsidizing local medical facilities (generally because foreign customers pay higher prices for procedures than local people).

Opponents say that cosmetic surgery overseas can take away resources from local health systems, especially in poorer countries where staff and facilities are badly needed to serve locals. They argue that cosmetic surgery in many countries is often unregulated and unsafe. Patients may not speak the local language and communication between doctor and patient may be restricted. Although an operation may appear to go well, complications appear only after the patient returns home. The result is that public health services back home may have to treat complications caused by infections and botched operations, often at the tax payer's expense.

It's a fact

In Japan and China, facial operations are popular, especially those that make the face more Western-looking. This includes creating rounder eyes, less prominent cheek muscles and dimples.

▲ A safari with a difference – 'Surgeon and Safari' holidays are popular in South Africa. They combine cosmetic surgery and a wildlife safari.

viewpoints

'Cosmetic surgery patients used to be a very elite group, very wealthy and high-status individuals who could afford to stay at their beach houses for a week to recuperate. Today they make up only 15-20 per cent of my practice. For the most part my patients are regular people who feel their self-confidence would improve if they just saved up a little money and worked on what's bothering them about their appearance.'

Dr Sarah Boyce, cosmetic dermatologist, University of Alabama, United States

'You are not going to have too many plastic surgeons saying you don't really need this. Once you get in the door of course the doctors are saying everything they can to persuade you to have surgery.'

Diana Zuckerman, National Center for Policy Research on Women and Families

summary

▶ With increasing demand worldwide, cosmetic surgery can be a very profitable business, but some clinics have used unethical business practices and unqualified staff.

▶ Consumer organizations say that cosmetic surgery business should be better regulated and some governments are introducing new restrictions.

▶ Cosmetic surgery is now a global phenomenon, with many people travelling to have cosmetic surgery abroad where it is cheaper.

CHAPTER 7

Society and cosmetic surgery

Does cosmetic surgery benefit society as a whole? There are no definitive answers. Ultimately, the answer will depend on the relative value that people place on individual choice, compared to a more collective view of society. The question can be considered in financial and resource terms and how it affects people's attitudes to age and beauty.

The costs to society

Both supporters and opponents agree that the rapid development of plastic surgery has brought huge benefits to individuals and to society. It means that people who were once fated to live their lives with features such as a cleft palate that made eating and drinking difficult, can have it removed or repaired in a regular operation.

Children like Lakshmi (see page 9), born with extra limbs or major deformities, now have the opportunity to lead pain-free and independent lives. A woman who has lost a breast to cancer can have a breast reconstruction. A burns victim can have a skin graft to restore his or her damaged and destroyed skin.

Many supporters see developments in cosmetic surgery as a natural outgrowth of advances in plastic surgery. If people's lives can be changed by repairing problems created by nature, accidents or in warfare, why should this knowledge not be used to aid people who want or feel the need to enhance or change their appearance? Supporters agree that not everyone will want to take advantage of what cosmetic

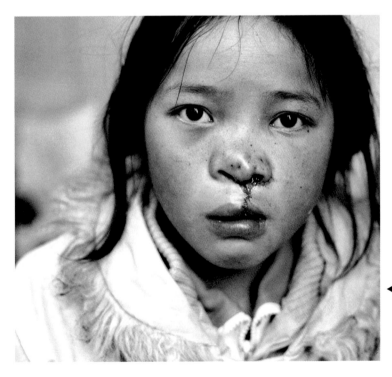

◀ Recovering from an operation to correct her cleft palate, this 11-year-old Chinese girl looks forward to a brighter future.

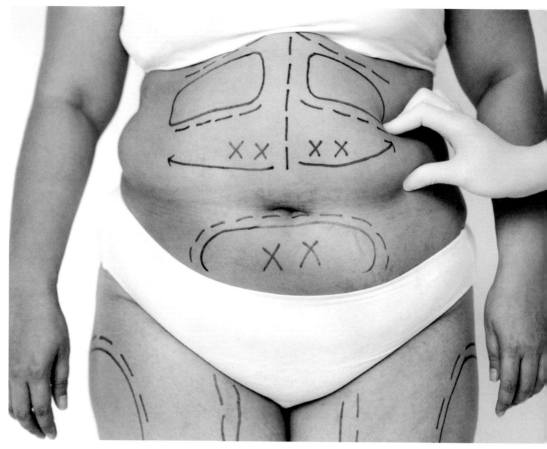

▲ X marks the spot – this patient has been marked up for the surgery that will remove excess skin and fat from her body in a major operation.

surgery has to offer but it should be a matter of individual choice. Falling costs mean that cosmetic surgery is now affordable for ever more people. Most people who opt for cosmetic surgery do so because they feel that it is important for their future health and happiness. There are many stories of individuals who say how much cosmetic surgery has changed their lives by enhancing their appearance and raising their confidence and self-esteem.

Opponents of cosmetic surgery say that it is a symbol of an unequal society and a waste of valuable resources and skills that could be used for necessary plastic surgery

or in other areas of medicine. They point out that both plastic and cosmetic surgery are developments of rich societies. While affluent women and men happily pay high prices for unnecessary cosmetic operations, in many poorer societies, children are unable to receive basic plastic surgery, such as repairing a cleft palate. Even in affluent countries, there is a huge gap between private clinics providing cosmetic surgery and overstretched public hospitals providing basic care. It is these same public health systems that end up picking up the costs of operations that have gone wrong and the physical and psychological problems that can result.

A contestant is prepared for the final of Miss Artificial Beauty, held in Beijing, China, in December 2004. The competition was open to women who had undergone cosmetic surgery and participants ranged in age from 62 to 17. Cosmetic surgery has become increasingly popular in China for young women, not just for aesthetic reasons but also because a beautiful face can help in landing a well-paid job.

A better society?

Supporters of cosmetic surgery argue that it is a matter of individual choice and therefore increases individual freedom and control. No longer do people have to live with the features with which they are born or that develop as they age. Cosmetic surgery allows people to enhance their faces and reshape their bodies. By changing their features, people can change their lives for the better. For example, individuals can go on to find a better job, a new partner or a stronger motivation in life. We live in an aspirational society and the growth of cosmetic surgery reflects those aspirations.

Critics see a society that is competitive and conformist, rather than aspirational and individualistic. Instead of giving people greater choice, cosmetic surgery helps to create dissatisfaction. People cannot accept

It's a fact

In 2007, the most sought-after medical specialities among US medical students were cosmetic surgery, dermatology (skin diseases) and otolaryngology (ear, nose and throat, also involving some plastic surgery). These were also some of the highest paying specialities.

that faces and bodies come in many shapes and sizes but aim to follow whatever look is dictated by current fashion trends, whether that is snub noses, large breasts, flat stomachs, or inward belly buttons, sometimes accumulating large debts in the process. As a result, many societies do not accept ageing and are often intolerant of imperfections, where quirkiness or individuality are discouraged and 'ugly' people are laughed at or shunned.

A path to happiness?

Does cosmetic surgery make people happier? Supporters say that it can make an enormous difference to individuals.

By raising their confidence and self-esteem, it improves their physical and emotional health and their relationship with family, friends and colleagues. Critics say that it is difficult to measure happiness and that if people are unhappy they can improve their lives in less radical and expensive ways. A society that uses cosmetic surgery does not really value people for what they are but for how they look, and that does not encourage happiness.

The extent and influence of cosmetic surgery is often overrated. After all, despite its worldwide growth, even in the richest countries only a minority of people opt to have cosmetic surgery. Most people decide that cosmetic surgery is not for them. A growing number of people will undertake some treatments, usually the cheaper, less invasive treatments, such as Botox, rather than surgical operations. A small number will resort to major surgery, sometimes again and again. Ultimately, it is up to individuals to decide whether cosmetic surgery is the right path for them to follow.

viewpoints

'These days the consumer can choose what to do with his hard-earned dosh: fork out for the new kitchen appliance, take the holiday in Bazaruto, or go for the snip, nip and tuck to take ten years off their face.'
Dr Dirk Lazarus, University of Cape Town, South Africa

'The clock is still going to run at the same rate that it's been running. Cosmetic surgery really doesn't stop or slow down the clock of ageing. All we can do is turn it back.'
Dr Jorge de la Torre, Center for Advanced Surgical Aesthetics, University of Alabama

summary

▶ Supporters say that society gains many benefits from cosmetic surgery but critics argue that it is a waste of valuable resources.

▶ Supporters state that cosmetic surgery supports individual choice and freedom.

▶ Opponents say that cosmetic surgery creates a conformist and intolerant society.

Glossary

Aesthetic fillers Collagen (see below) and fat (usually from the patient's own body), injected into the facial skin to improve skin texture.

Anaesthetic A substance that causes loss of sensation or unconsciousness, used in surgical operations and in dentistry.

Body dysmorphic disorder (BDD) A form of mental illness whereby a person is obsessed with a supposed defect in their appearance.

Chemical peels Removing outer layers of the skin using chemicals, to smooth the skin and remove freckles, sunspots and uneven pigmentation.

Cleft palate A birth defect whereby a baby is born with a division in the mouth and/or lips, which can be corrected by early surgery.

Collagen A protein found in the body, commonly used in treatment for burns victims and in cosmetic surgery.

Cosmetic surgery Operations or procedures that revise or change the appearance, colour, texture, structure or position of body features that would otherwise be considered 'normal'.

Exploitative Used selfishly, to make a profit at someone's expense.

Hippocratic Oath A code of ethics in ancient Greece, stating principles that should govern the conduct of doctors towards their patients, which has influenced the code of ethics for modern medical practice.

Implant/implant sac Something that is put under the skin or implanted to increase size or improve shape. It usually refers to silicone sacs filled with saline used in breast or buttock implants.

Injectables Treatments administered by injection, such as collagen.

Laser treatment Removing upper layers of skin using a laser, a beam of light radiation.

Plastic surgery A branch of surgery, specializing in repairing, replacing and rebuilding damaged or diseased faces and bodies through operations, including skin grafts and reshaping features.

Principles Doctrine or guidelines used as a guide to action.

Psychological Referring to the mind, for example a psychological illness is one that originates in the way a person thinks or feels about something, rather than having a physical cause.

Public health systems Clinics, hospitals and other health facilities owned and run by the government to benefit the public, usually free of charge or at low cost.

Reconstructive Rebuilding or repairing, as opposed to cosmetic or superficial.

Regulation Rules that govern an industry or a practice, usually agreed and inspected by a government agency or a trade association.

Self-esteem The belief a person has in themselves and their ability to face the world and to interact with other people. Also known as self-respect.

Silicone A type of strong plastic, formerly used for breast implant filling.

Therapy A non-invasive treatment, usually to treat mental or emotional illnesses or problems, such as talking to a therapist alone or attending meetings with people with similar problems.

Timeline

1846 The first public demonstration of a surgical operation in Boston Massachusetts using ether is followed by rapid adoption of the new technique of anaesthetics during surgery in the United States and Europe.

1914 onwards Reconstructive plastic surgery to aid injured solders and victims of war is developed.

1940 onwards Further progress is made in reconstructive plastic surgery, including skin grafts to aid injured solders and victims of war.

1960s Silicone-filled breast implants are introduced in the United States.

1992 The US Food and Drug Administration (FDA) stops sale and use of silicone-filled breast implants. Bans later follow in the United States and many other countries around the world.

1994 Three major manufacturers of silicone-filled breast implants agree to pay US$3.7 million (£1.85 million) to women made ill by silicone implants.

1997 Over two million cosmetic surgery procedures are carried out in the United States.

2002 Almost seven million cosmetic surgery procedures are carried out in the United States.

2005 An expert committee reports to the UK Chief Medical Officer, recommending tighter regulation of cosmetic surgery in the UK, especially in marketing and public information.

2006 Nearly 11 million cosmetic surgery procedures are carried out in the United States.

2007 Over 11.7 million cosmetic procedures are carried out in the United States, at a total cost of US$13.2 billion (£6.5 billion).

Further information

Books:

Cosmetic Surgery (Science in the News)
Andrew Campbell
(Franklin Watts 2008)

Body Sculpting: Science at the Edge
Sally Morgan (Franklin Watts, 2008)

Websites:

www.changingfaces.org.uk
TeensHealth provides answers and advice on health and social issues and there is a section on cosmetic surgery.

www.dh.gov.uk/en/Publichealth/CosmeticSurgery/index.htm
Information and advice on cosmetic surgery from the UK Department of Health.

www.channel4.com/health/microsites/L/lust4life/index.html
Lust4Life – Linked to a UK television station, this website has information on cosmetic surgery, diet and exercise.

www.which.co.uk/campaigns/cosmetic-treatments/index.jsp
Which? – the Uk's leading consumer organization has carried out several investigations into cosmetic surgery..

Index

Numbers in **bold** refer to illustrations.

Ethical Debates

Contents of new titles in the series:

Animal Research and Testing
978 0 7502 4818 1

Birth Control
978 0 7502 5657 5

Cosmetic Surgery
978 0 7502 5654 4

Energy Resources
978 0 7502 5658 2

Euthanasia
978 0 7502 56551

Tourism
978 0 7502 5656 8

WAYLAND